EXIT MOO

Also by Joy Howard

SECOND BITE
(with Hilary J Murray and Gina Shaw)

A TWIST OF MALICE (ed)

EXIT MOONSHINE

Coming Out and Carrying On

Joy Howard

First published in 2009 by Grey Hen Press
PO Box 450
Keighley
West Yorkshire
BD22 9WS
www.greyhenpress.com

ISBN 978-0-9552952-0-1

Printed by Q3 Digital/Litho, Loughborough, Leicestershire LE11 1LE

For all of us, but especially the late-comers, who sometimes have to run very fast to catch up…

How chance Moonshine is gone before Thisbe comes back and finds her lover?

Shakespeare: *A Midsummer Night's Dream*

About this publication

In 1981, at the age of 40, my life turned upside down when I made
the astounding discovery that I had been a lesbian all along, and as if
in celebration began taking poetry seriously and writing lots of it.
This book is a selection representative of the subsequent journey, and
most of the poems belong to that time. But as nothing much changes
in the search for love and a sense of belonging, they are presented in
the hope that everyone who has experienced the fear and thrill of
finding a new identity, or just falling in (and out of) love will find
something that strikes a chord.

Joy Howard

Acknowledgements

Several of these poems were first published in the following anthologies:

Beautiful Barbarians, Onlywomen Press 1986; *Dancing the Tightrope,* The Women's Press 1987; *Naming the Waves* Virago 1988; *Not For The Academy,* Onlywomen Press 1997; *A Twist of Malice,* Grey Hen Press 2008

Grey Hen Press
PO Box 269
Kendal
Cumbria
LA9 9FE

With Compliments

Phone: 01539 731175
Email: info@greyhenpress.com
Website: www.greyhenpress.com

+ all good wishes - thanks for the trip back to the 80's

Contents

Will She, Won't She….

This Must Be Love

That'll Be The Day

Some Nights

Beyond Casablanca

Envoi

Will She, Won't She...?

The Lesser Id

I'm a large(ish) person
tall enough to reach top shelves
at fourteen (plus) already hunching my
shoulders at the back of the back row
bruising easy   but a voice
that always had me out
in the corridor first   even though
thirty others were all talking
at the same time

Now forty (plus)   I'll cry out rivers
reach round cities
laugh till my ribs crack
dance till dawn
and still there's a small
rather anxious   shy
and tentative person
inside of me   trying
to creep
out

Audition

Here I stand
not knowing what to do
with my hands
not touching you
nor how to stop my heart
from leaping to my mouth
and giving tongue
to my desire
so dumb
and frozen   I am left
not finding voice enough
for the aria
with only the whisper
of a song
the echo of a dream

Well I mean to say
I never was cut out
for operatic glitter
it's not my scene
happiest among my jokes
I'm fitter
for a stand-up comedy
routine

Sissinghurst

'When I close my eyes I see
bluebells'   she said
remembering what?   a wander
through the coppiced trees
a laugh   a touch
a wondering whether we – or not –

Or maybe she
was thinking of the view
while you
were seeing more in woods
of bluebells
than you should

Will She, Won't She...

Maybe today
I'll say how much
you know
and why I never
up till now
and well you see you are
to me
and I shall
oh well what
the hell
I might as well
it can't
be worse
than more of this
      god
         awful
            verse

What, a Play Toward!

Funny wasn't it   how you
and I   like actors
teased and joked away our time
going for laughs
with now and then a little edge
to it – of competition?
rivalry?   or was it some sharper arrow
deflecting from our fathers'
chambered wall?

A good script though   well learned
(with just an occasional prompt)
reliable   could have
a long run
always all right
on the night

What puckish demon
was it then that made me
call you 'darling'
(did you hear it?)
bound to blunt you   a stone
falling by accident
dangerous   a gap
that had to be closed

Oh yes   stone walls
still need repairing
in this country   built
with chinks just wide enough
for moonshine
not the hoarse-whispered blurtings
of a blundering Thisbe
with a fear

of forgetting her lines
and half an eye
for Hippolyta

Always in trouble with my timing
lion stage-fright snarling
in the wings
forgive me then if I
(in rustic confusion)
sometimes wished
to toss the script and leap the wall
and exit moonshine
with a kiss?

North Country

In the strange shock
of silence
chilling the house
new sensations
swoop and swirl
in endlessly changing
old formations
like swallows on the moor
unable to decide
whether to stay
or if it's time
to leave for Africa

Tetrahedron

I

Oh come   Pandora   surely you
can bring yourself to
open me
a crack
come now   aren't you a little
interested?
don't you feel   amidst
your understandable anxiety
a small sweet shiver   a desire
to know
what's in me?

I am just
a plain undecorated casket
insignificant   one among many
only if you choose me
shall I have earned
capital letters   you
might give me a name   I could
be known
down endless ages as
Pandora's Box
imagine that

Together
we could be famous
are we to remain   merely
a faintly curious but hesitant
woman   and six square sides
of unvarnished wood?

You ask me what you're
in for?
I can't tell you   only say
on cool grey days I feel

the faint uneasy
stirrings
of a high wind coming
from the west
a warmth from occasional sun
like the seeds
of huge tropical trees
a dampness in the air
that could turn
into torrents
and a distant rumble
of thunder
that's all   and it may of course
be nothing

If nothing   well then I'm still
a useful if rather ordinary
container
and yours   if you need me
if all   why
Pandora   we may
discover Atlantis or drown
in the venture

Come then   turn
the lock
fling your caution
to the four winds
I only ask   think
twice   before you
throw away the key

II

Ever since Eve   I've known
the dangers of curiosity
only they never taught me
how

to put out the burning
you're right   I am tormented
with thirst for your secrets

This key?   well I found
it by accident   some
sly guard must have left it
lying about on purpose
to tempt me
look how it gleams
dully in my shaded
palm   how it twirls
restless in my fingers

Here I stand   uncertain
with your smooth dark
wood   caressing my hand
your little lock inlaid
with pearl
inviting my touch

It should be so easy   why
do I feel as though
the fate of the world waited
on my decision   I am only
Pandora   daughter
of the dry mountains
and lover
of the sea

And you?   only a small
box   animal
vegetable and mineral
and not fearful
or only a little
of the fiercer elements

So you too want to try
for Atlantis?   and maybe
like me   you don't go

for package tours
and we may not get this chance
again   true enough
and the key
shall go with us
I will wear it with
my amulets   and it shall never
leave us

Be ready   yes
I am coming

III

So you think do you
both of you
that I
am yours
that I belong
in a lock
that I will be kept
as an amulet?

Beware!   I am not
for possessing
I am small   but
slippery
I shine   but I do not
lead the way

And while each of you
searches
for the Lost City
I may
quietly drop
through a crack among the rocks
between the roots of a tree
into the foam of the waves

under a coverlet of fine sand
gone
for good
leaving you to make
the best of your own ways
home

Whatever happens   do not say
I never told you so

IV

Look to the sea
sun-flecked
unguessable
Atlantis
is mine

This Must Be Love

The Pearl Hunter

I'm diving deeper
soon
there'll be no heading
back for the surface
and I
merwoman
weaving among the weeds
haunting the coral caves
with my soundless cry
and sightless tears
will mourn
for the sport of the shallows

Would You Tell Me?

I don't know what
the fullness of your welcome
is offering

or what your steady gaze
is measuring

I couldn't calculate how much
of sisterhood was in your kiss

or gauge the full tog rating
of your quilted voice

I don't know which
direction it might be you're
pointing

and if it's by-roads or
the motorway

I can't say if your North
is a magnetic or a true one

or how you travel whether
light or loaded

gilt or gold   I don't know which
you're minting
street lamp or star   I don't know which
is glinting   and if your forte's marathon
or sprinting

but I know I'd like
to find out

Love Poem

How delightful it is to love you
it is like curling up in a warm bed
on a winter's night
finding a last rose of summer
in a cold corner of the garden
or a box of chocolates on a shelf
that were for someone's birthday two weeks ago

or on another level
like waking in the morning to find
the leaking cistern fixed
broken windows mended
new lino on the kitchen floor
twenty pairs of matching socks
in my son's drawer

now who would have thought that socks
could ever be a metaphor for love?
maybe only another
mother

Mornings After

Now
that I'm missing your
hands' touch
wishing I hadn't got
so used to you
that it should hurt
to have you simply
not with me
thinking   my fault
for letting you
get such a hold upon
my heart
hating the light
hurting my eyes
reaching
for the shade
I start to write and yes
already I'm more anxious
for the touch of my
typewriter
and the heart
aches
fade

poetica interrupta

Lying in the cool
and quiet dark
long after midnight
lapped in tiredness
letting languor
steal over my senses
holding her head
upon my shoulder
as above the waves
drifting into sleep
and thinking
of this poem
I felt her soft hands light
upon my skin like fronds
of seaweed stroking
my underwater limbs
turning night into day
quiescence to quickening
water to fire

Next day her morning
voice saying
'how did that happen? I will
remember bit by bit'
I didn't tell her I was working
on the poem   even before
anything did

Habitats

In a tangle
of soft brown hair
though I
skim over days
silky-petalled
glide past time
on a clover breath
float through the race
on a swan's feather
trace the lines of my life
along lily stems
I end and begin
in a bramble
of red brown hair
born and bred
in a briar patch

This must be love because I feel so unwell

Sometimes
when I want to write a poem
I find
everything's been said
by the time
I've written the title

it's just that

if it wasn't (love that is)
I wouldn't be so worried sick
that it might not be
would I?

Wanting You

Not at all
the peaceful picture
I gave you earlier
I'm pacing
up and down
while waiting
for your call
pausing to perch
on my piano stool
and gaze for just
a moment at
the empty sofa
filling in the blanks
with you   like
I've been doing
all day

In all my empty spaces
you've been there
and I can't remember
life before yesterday

Reaching Consensus

A lengthy process
and hard work
though definitely the right
thing to do

So we talked for quite a long time
about a good many things
drank a few glasses of wine
shared a meal and some ideas
and so on

In agreement
on most of the quite
substantial
agenda   to date   we reached
inevitably but rather
later than we might have
any other business
as so often the main item
of the evening
in this case your
place or mine

Now
to take care
of any matters arising

Vanilla Sugar

Vanilla sugar
sweetie pie
no-one more in love
than I

cinnamon cookie
honey bun
you and I have so
much fun

we've no wish for
stronger spices
tricks and traps and
strange devices

we can never
get enough
of the other
kind of stuff

so peppermint candy
sweet cachou
you eat me and I'll
eat you

Metropolitan Lines

The grey train
I thought would never get going
now chugs complacently
through vast suburban sprawls
with ancient and outlandish
names   like Ruislip Manor
Ickenden
and Harrow-on-the-Hill

Who knows
what stories lie beneath
neat winter gardens and the sea
of three beds two receps and a garage
pre-and-post war semis
in what isn't even
Middlesex
any more   but only
an anonymous
Outer London Borough

Metroland
isn't what it was
and what it was before
and before that
you could wonder till the cows
that used to graze here
came home   which would be
a long time

Arriving   eventually
at Uxbridge
(no sign of a river
and a railway the only
bridge in sight)
picked up by a minicab
outside SupaSnaps
transported to a yellow ugly
institution   worse

to a cancelled meeting
a wasted journey
a tedious return
I call you (to see if you're
home)   and the grey train
suddenly painted red
has me inside the heart of the city
in seconds   I'm back
at Baker Street and heading
for the Jubilee
and Central
lines

Flowery Verse

You are tired of gazing
into my garden through a haze
of acid rain (it's been a long
winter) so now I'll write you
poems like peonies
lush and lovely spilling out words
like rounded petals
bursting from tight fat buds
untinged by lemon

A guest appearance
by the prima donnas of the border
tucked and frilled in foamy pink
swathed in sheeny satin red
and glowing curled to frame a golden
throat and billowing
in silky swirls of double cream
they sweep the stage in high
herbaceous glory

In the unexpected flood
of sunlight kissed
in unaccustomed heat
we can choose not to hear
the thunderclap
that brings on rain again

We have deserved
a bit of summer

That'll Be The Day

Undertow

I think I have discovered
how to love
without possessing
and in tenderness
my life caressing
yours   and each of us
our own still pool
whose outward ripples
break and return again
to secret and untroubled depths

I never reckon with
the wild water creatures
that swim beneath
until I touch you
and the peaceful centre stirs
divides and trembles
as diving for the deep
goes the silver darting fish
of desire

Casablanca Time Again

Shall I have to spend the
                     rest of my life
      saying tearful goodbyes
                     at airports
    my first flight I cried
             at take-off and on landing
    I couldn't understand it – now
                I see it as an omen
another plane   another year   another love
       another tear   another goddam
         airport
              goodbye

You can't go to the Moon there's no Trains

To wish
for the moon
is so unrealistic
why   when there is
a whole round shining earth
to wander
should I dream
of a gleaming chimera
I should be content
to catch her bright reflection
in a pool
and leave her be
delighting in
her mystery
not long
for mastery
politically as well as
poetically
undesirable

Unrequited – a Haiku

Always on my mind
and never where I want you
into my body

Fantasy

Dreamer of impossible dreams
with the warm winds
of the South
floating my hair
and the flashing waters
of Northern hills
sparkling my skin
I want beauty
love   rainbows
the sun stars and moon
and for you to arrive
      on time
          just
              once

On Call

The phone rings and pulls me
like a netted fish   reluctant
struggling to stay in the sea   and how
I needed to be asleep
this night   but I fall
out of the net and into
the feathered softness of your voice
and turn into
one of those silly ducklings
who identifies
the first moving living thing it sees
as its   mother / guide / mentor
and will paddle around after her
all day

So before I can stop myself   I am
rolling in feathers again
and making little cheeping noises
of joy and contentment
when what I should be doing
is giving you my
prepared speech
my platformed dignity

How like you
to home in on me this way
when my defences have been downed
in sleep   a difficult day
and a couple of gins

How like me
when I have sworn
on the heads of my past lovers
never to come near

your little finger   again
to let myself be twisted
like yarn from the fleece
around your spindle

I do protest   but it's too late
already the weaving has started
there is a pattern   familiar
emerging in the fabric
old jokes   like diamonds
form in the weft
in no time it seems
we have our magic carpet
once more at our feet

This time   please
not Xanadu

That'll Be The Day

One day
I'll have shed my last tear
over you

One day
we'll have kissed for the last
time

One day
I'll wake up not thinking
about you

And one day you
won't care

Cutting Edge

I like my poems better now
less imagery
sharper
more honest
and direct
like pain

But I will like them better still
when I can write
in more removed
and philosophical a style
love you dear and let you go
with a wry smile

I Could Really Love a Woman

Who
eats when she's hungry and not for
any other reason   and then gets it
over with as quickly as possible
except for Mars bars

Who understands the delicate
unbreakable nature of the relationship
between hot water bottles and cold
feet

Who occupies both sides
of the bed   and takes all
the duvet

Who knows about the soothing properties
of mashed potatoes
soft-boiled egg sandwiches
port-and-brandy and tinned
rice pudding

Who can really take care of me
because of knowing all these things
and a hundred more

Why don't I fling my arms round
her and dance off
into the sunset?   Well
it's hard to waltz with oneself
and not spill the cocoa

And I have to admit that with me
though regular   and on demand
and just how I like it and all that
the sex   like the conversation
tends to get a bit predictable
after a while

Another Learning Experience

I've given up
red roses
violets
valentines

and taken up
sleeping
eating
and watching TV

I'm giving up
therapy
weeping
and working it out

and taking up
typing out
old
poems

I'm definitely cured
of romanticism
at least
until
I fall in love
again

Some Nights

Honeysuckle

I drowse in the warmth of velvet skin
and wake to eyes deep brimming
I sway to the gentle weight of your limbs
while you brush my face with bee's-wing hands
and bring me back to the morning

Take me to your humming hive
and make me honey
a golden drop of sun to thrive
in a secret scented cell
alive
for winter's coming

Winter Clothing

You own
a heavy coat
at twenty pounds
too weighty
for an English winter

It hangs
unseen in your cupboard
but I can feel the heft
for there's its fellow
hanging from your shoulders
reaching to your toes
enclosing you
in dark impenetrable folds
protection from a possible
cold snap

The weather here is
unpredictable   and has
a nasty habit
of creeping up on you
invading your cosy living
room   even
your kitchen
even your
bed

But you've
your coat   silent   thick
wide-spreading   covering
the floor   occupying all available
air   defying
any weather in the world
to get you

And still
I wonder if   inside
of there   you're managing
to keep warm

Mnemonics

Through a long cold city Spring
we've courted one another   watched
each other   I have felt
your gaze upon my body   I've
observed you   and I know we hold
our images
behind each shuttered eye   can print
each other out on stiff white
paper when we will
our faces   gestures and the dear
difficult habitual ways we walk
hard city pavements

But there's a different place to be
some old abandoned shore
whose warm gulf waters' breaking waves
explore the rocks with gentle runneling
fingers of foam   persistent
patient   fierce with ancient need
to know each crack   each crevice
every tiny barnacle and strand
of seaweed   till the tide sucks slowly
away   like the end of an embrace
a memory as intimate as womb-water
and deep as the pulse of the sea

Enclosure

What is the matter with you?
my keeper says   why
do you have to be so emotional?
she says
(and here in fairness I should add
that I was acquiescent in my capture
even asked for it)

but now   dear guardian
when it's too late for a return
to the wild
since I have become sufficiently
institutionalised
and fear the dark   and not
knowing where the next meal
is coming from
I would appreciate
if not my freedom
then at least some sympathy
for my dilemma

or else transfer me
to some deeper hiding place
where I won't get a whiff
of the cold north wind
or a prickling of frost on pines
and a change of diet so
I don't have to remember
the forest at feeding time

otherwise don't act surprised
when you hear
the cage bars rattle
and the welcoming wolves
howl

Los Angeles, December

We knew her well
in dark or shining
her phases we recorded
lovingly   our tides
flowed with each wax and wane

Now on this
unfamiliar planet
with my camera eye
focussed to infinity   I gaze
on a total eclipse of the moon

London, June

As I wake from a dream of the sun
fine light rain is falling
a cold mist of days
still follows the storm
and the heart-wreck

In the huddle and shiver of light
struggling for warmth
drawn in against the damp
I feel the bone-bending
age-old aching of English days
unreached by summer

Expedition

Set to search the glory and the source
of Northern Lights
we started trekking
made light of our load and sang
our stepping easy

Soon we left behind sweet Arctic spring
soft tundra mosses   lichen
birdsong   ground-hugging flora
reached the permafrost

Bitter blizzards
obscured a waning sunlight
and the deep snows
of a silent wasteland
became our home

Over the creaking ice
we stumbled
dreading the green depths
of each crevasse
faint heart never won
we said   and tried to warm
frost-bitten hands and faces
by the fading flame of our
last lamp

Defeated   numb with cold
we watched once more the wild
dawn dance of the Borealis
saw in our mind's eye only
an artificial sunburst
and turned our tracks forever
into night

Some Nights

In the middle of some night
empty   I might ache
to touch you
and find peace in the smooth of your skin
sleep in the stroke of your hair

some night I might
miss you

Some thick-curtained night
fierce   I might rage
through the dark
and fling back in the burn of my fire
the bright brand you hand me

some night I might
hurt you

Some soft-pillowed night
gentle   I will come
to kiss you
and float free on the unanchored deep
safe in the drift of our tide

through the middle of some night
I will love you

Heat Loss

One night of summer and I've held you
limp with heat   asleep   in my arms
and all I want is to hold you like this
no more   poetry   I'm thinking
it's a lonely business   give me love
any day

Waking it seems   the season's changed
again   outside it's raining
I want you still   you've gone
and here am I   another bloody poem
taking cold shape under my hands
that only want the rhythms
of your body   and another
summer's night

'All through the wasteland night'

All through the wasteland night
I wandered starless wondering to be
a living creature still among
no others and not die
a dreamless sleep escaping though I lay
quiet for the catching   would not fly
from her and yet she kept away
while soft and soundless tears were flowing
in little rivers never deep enough for drowning
she swam beside me sorrowful
but would not stay

Sinking at last I slept but dreaming
woke in the lost land   still
I could not find my way   then you
came with the dawn
and suddenly as sunrise   turned
my desolation into day

Old Acquaintance

Lust   my old friend   where
are you? I've thought I haven't
needed you   in fact I've been thinking of you
as getting to be a bit of a tiresome nuisance
always popping round and demanding a cup
of sugar   twist of salt   spoonful of honey
in fact I've rather begun to dread your knock
sending a small lurch through my pulse and into the pit
of my stomach

Once you used to make me feel alive
now you remind me I'm growing older   needing
my store cupboard filled with sweet preserves
especially in these days of tightening belts
with rationing upon us again

Getting down to it I've been quite angry with you
you've caused   a lot of trouble between
me and her   she doesn't like you
finds you too insistent   too intense
I've had to bolt the door on you   not hear you
make you go away

Of course I miss you sometimes
as I hold her   soft and smelling of roses
but I've got to stop wanting to plunder
her shelves   empty her store   or what with you
and me arriving after dark and into devouring everything
there'll be nothing left for winter

But now that your perseverance has become
so faint and uninsistent   look what's happening
I miss you   I want you
banging at my door like there's no tomorrow
I want to sit you at my table   feast in abandon
fall to   like the nights were not
drawing in

It's come to this   I think I owe you an apology
it doesn't do to give up on old friends for
a lover   maybe in time she'll grow to like you
so when you next come calling (I'll know it's you)
I promise to be there   and please
would you make it soon?

Beyond Casablanca

Launch
(*at The Poetry Society*)

In the society
of a poet

wanting the
society of
another

reading a poem
about transience
betrayal   love and
goodbyes

feeling a heel
and flying
like a kite

this is the
kind of high
society   poetry
can get you into

Monstrosities

I know you
we've met before
I'm in your eyes   and in
the running current
of your blood   we
are the trolls that live under
the bridge
older than rivers   wiser
than goats
they fear us   call us
monsters
do not see   the beast
is beauty
and the green grass of the meadow
only a fable

Beyond Casablanca

Journeying in high-born company
the pride of the desert
we come to an early oasis
not a scheduled stop   the riders
make to pass by
noses in air and haughty
cheeks averted
no betrayal
of the cause   no weakness
death
were preferable

Me   I rein in my camel
joyously   seeing dying as no
great shakes
careless of tomorrow's possible
transactions
today
is my business

We exchange one look   farewell
the caravan
the noble purpose of our journey
dust   I see
the promise in your golden eye
and know that travelling
to Samarkand
goes on wherever there's you and me
and water

Only You

I think of you and want to sing
lines of huge moment
wide encircling sweeps of sea
great symphonies of wind and weather
my skies filled with mountains
and my land watered with streams

But this is not the stuff of poetry
no raindrop distillation
of a perfect poignant moment
no jarring bite on stone
at the heart of the fruit

So there is only you

Only a riotous plenty
a dear concordance and
a priceless peace

Champagne and Cocoa

From the first   it was like that
fizz and familiarity

now here we sit   twenty years on
armchaired

hands curved round warm cups
bubbles rising

Envoi

Section 28

All right you've got me
frightened   and
I promise I won't
proselytise

But you can't stop me
walking down the street like an ad
for the Reverend Gentleman's
Fresh Air Fund   you see
country life
brings a glow to my cheeks
and a sparkle
to my eyes   like down
in the Fighting Cocks
never did

And you'd better make outbreaks
of happiness
a notifiable disease
for I'm telling you
it's catching as hell

Not a Poet
(for Sheila Jeffreys)

Why can't we talk properly
about our lovers?
she asked me   meaning (of course)
improperly
why are we all so silent?
well I said   there's always
Poetry (and coughed a little nervously not
wanting to advertise)
do you ever...?
oh no she said quite
forcefully (not a poet   no)
I was thinking yesterday
she went on   of how
my lover's skin smells
like the sun was on it   and her hair
that smells too
of the sun...
but never a poet   she
oh no

Nature / Nurture
(for Irene Weiss)

A sad sight is a row
of pollarded willows
maturing in confinement
for ever kept
from finding their true form
young growth constantly
cut down
woven and distorted
into useful household articles

Sometimes   years later
worn out   battered
seen as useless
thrown
into a ditch
stuck
in the ground
a dried out wand
may start behaving
like a young cutting
put out
tentative roots
feel
the sap start to flow
come Spring
new leaf is budding
there is life
in the old wood yet

But such late springing
can never quite produce
the perfect form
of the untrained willow
whose early pliancy

unpruned
is still seen
in her utmost branches
while her deep roots
feed
the firm and flowing
beauty
of her age

Prufrock Revisited

Oh yes I once went in for
measuring my life with coffee spoons
and toast and tea
I did not dare presume nor want
to play Prince Hamlet
walked on beaches never reaching for
the red-brown sea

(supposing she should say no that is
not what I meant
not it at all)

but there was time indeed
grown older now I wear
the bottoms of my trousers rolled like
any other dyke and eat
my daily peach
you see I hear
the mermaids singing each to each
and know
they sing for me

Joy Howard is a co-founder of Grey Hen Press. Her poems have featured in several anthologies (see Acknowledgements). She is a contributor to Grey Hen's first publication *Second Bite*. This is also the name of a group of three older women poets, of which Joy is a founder member, who give readings together. After a long career in social services, she is now re-focusing her energy on poetry. Shortlisted in several competitions, she was a Chapter One Open Poetry prizewinner in 2007, and has been published in *Sofia* and *Sphinx*. Her poems can be found online at *Guardian Unlimited* and *poetry p f,* and feature in 'Poems While You Wait' at St James's Hospital in Leeds. Her work has been selected for a new anthology from Headland Publications in 2009.

www.greyhenpress.com